# She Says, *It's Complicated!*

### Volume I

# She Says, It's Complicated!

## Volume I

*Simple Solutions for Women in Complex Relationships with Men*

## SHELBY M. HILL MBA CPC
### RELATIONSHIP SPECIALIST

Foreword by Carol Ross

**SEED WORD COMMUNICATIONS**

**She Says, It's Complicated!**
Copyright ©2010 by Shelby M. Hill

ISBN 978-0-9817603-5-3

Published by:
Seed Word Communications
P.O. Box 16615
Tallahassee, FL 32317
Phone: +1.850.765.0386
www.seedword.com

Cover design: Johnny T. Chirse
Branding and IT integration: Jaoo Studios
contact@jaoostudios.info
Phone: 704.806.4223

Interior design and copyediting: Alan Prescott
prescott_alan@comcast.net
alanjayprescott@gmail.com
prescottdesignshop.com
Phone: 949.412.4548

# dedication

*I* dedicate this book to my mom, Sylvia; my sister, Lisa; and my loving wife, British. I am most grateful for all of their nurturing love and guidance. They have unconditionally embraced my evolution into manhood and my ongoing journey in life. I can only hope all men experience love from such an invaluable spectrum of God's gift to mankind. Women give us breath...embrace them.

# foreword

Relationships are *complicated*—so we say. Relative to our definitions of them, our experiences comply with our innermost beliefs. Like the heart pumping blood throughout our veins, our belief system is the central command center that pumps out our reactions to everything we experience in relation to others. While the heart controls the circulatory system, our beliefs control our perceptions.

From childhood on, our belief systems develop and become the "blueprints" we rely on to navigate our choices in life. How we relate—and subsequently how *complex* we deem our relationships to be—is determined or heavily influenced by that initial blueprint. But is the complexity of a relationship real or imagined? Is it self-perpetuated or an innocent victim of circumstance? And what components actually prompt us to call it *complicated*? What would seem completely impossible to one could be an entirely exciting adventure to another. How we view our relationships lies in our expectations, and our expectations most likely trace back to—you guessed it—our blueprints. What if we could redraw our blueprints? By stepping out of the comfort of our automatic reactions and expectations, we have an opportunity to change the angle from which we view our lives for a more expanded experience. By altering our expectations with a broader viewpoint, we have now gained control of our blueprints. We are now in the driver's seat and can go in any direction we choose. What does all of that mean? It means relationships are *complicated*...only if that's what we choose them to be.

The moment I met Shelby Hill, I had a sense that I'd met him before. It wasn't the kind of familiarity you would equate with just having walked past someone at the grocery store the day before. It was a familiarity in spirit—an immediate understanding that lives are made up of connections between souls and expansions of perspectives. That kindred recognition became more apparent as I got to know him. My conversations with Shelby created a connection between us and expanded my perception of relationships. During our talks, we circled the simplicity of life and discussed how we control its complexity by our daily choices. It is clear to me that Shelby Hill possesses a deeper understanding of the purpose of love in our collective lives.

As a woman, I realize how many of our sisters struggle daily to complete their lives. We are taught at an early age that much of our completion lies in the success of our relationships with men. We watch the clock that society places around our necks and pray that time lends a kind hand in our fate. But with an open mind and willing heart, we can expand our view and see how our lives change once we connect to a powerful source—ourselves.

In *She Says, It's Complicated!* Shelby takes us by the hand and walks with us along our own paths, gently pointing out where some of our choices potentially lead. He speaks to our hearts and reminds us that our power source comes from within. He shows us how our external experiences mirror who we are, revealing that complex relationships with others are really just reflections of the complex relationships we have with ourselves. Lending a male perspective, he gives us glimpses of the inner workings of the male psyche, allowing us to step back and see men from various angles. Through a question-and-answer approach, Shelby Hill honestly answers some of our most intimate questions with compassion and candor.

Born of organic introspection, Shelby Hill's warm and insightful guidance stirs the soul, encouraging us to seek deeper fulfillment in our relationships—he zeros in and makes it plain. With profound contemplation, he skillfully uses his knowledge in a way that challenges our core beliefs. An advocate for life's myriad opportunities for happiness, his desire to empower women is genuine. A shoulder to lean on, Shelby Hill's embrace is like having a best friend in a book.

Carol Ross
*Photographer and author*
carol@carolrossphotographer.com
www.carolrossphotographer.com

*Photographer and author Carol Ross published her debut book,* POP: A Celebration of Black Fatherhood, *with a forward by Samuel L. Jackson. An Essence Magazine Literary Award Finalist in Photography,* POP *was featured in* O Magazine, Heart & Soul, Baby Talk, Essence, The Washington Post, the Chicago Tribune *cover,* Advertising Age *and others. Ross's photographs have also appeared in* Ebony, VIBE, The Village Voice *and were published in the book* 73 Ways to Help Your Baby Sleep. *Ross has made guest appearances on* ABC 7 Chicago, Your Morning on CN8, Oprah & Friends Radio *and* WVON Chicago. *Her images have been exhibited at Gallery Guichard in Chicago; the Engaging Men 2009 Symposium in Rio de Janeiro, Brazil; the Augusta Savage Gallery at the University of Massachusetts; and the Franklin Institute in Philadelphia. She is currently working on her second photography book featuring relationships.*

# praise

*L*ife is way too short—and the sooner you read, absorb and apply this book, the better, simpler, more fun, exciting, personally inspiring and satisfying your life will become.

The fact that you are here reading these words now tells me that you've already realized time and life are far too valuable to toss any more of them away, wasted on unfulfilling, unproductive and unhealthy relationships with the types of men who *appear* to be everything you want. In the end, they deliver nothing but sadness, pain, frustration, heartaches and possibly a bad case of cynicism and low self-esteem.

So now you ask yourself, *Why this particular book—and why now?* That's a very wise question. Here's what I can tell you from my professional perspective, academic and research experience, and very personal journeys and adventures dealing directly in these matters over the past 30 years.

In those three decades, I have written and worked in close association with literally hundreds of genuinely well-intentioned, wise, insightful, educated, experienced and world-renowned doctors, therapists, universities, coaches, teachers, mentors and researchers. All of these individuals and institutions are involved in the precious process of helping people to better understand and deepen their relationships with others as well as themselves.

Whether the ultimate goal is to help others learn to come to a deeper, more authentic and meaningful relationship with their inner self, co-workers, team members—or, as in this case, helping women to fully understand, completely come to terms with and actually put into practice the various valuable tools and tips necessary to effectively develop deeper, better, healthier and much more satisfying relationships with the men in their lives—in the end it all comes down to self awareness and personal growth as a human being.

This is precisely what I love about working with Shelby Hill. Shelby has that very rare ability—dare I call it a unique talent and gift—of con-

sistently and continuously maintaining his understanding that it is all about remaining 100% authentically true to oneself, and thoroughly human
in the process.

Shelby is always a great and easy read, because
he neither tries to bedazzle you with complex
mental and verbal gymnastics, nor ever wastes
time trying to impress you with the vast complexity and comprehensiveness of his ideas, teachings
and personal/professional consciousness.

Shelby talks to his readers as though he is
comfortably sitting there with them, face to face,
heart to heart, having a beer or possibly a glass of
wine, a cup of coffee or perhaps you prefer tea.
The experience of reading Shelby Hill is that of a
close, occasionally intimate, personal conversation
with a dear and trusted friend!

What makes Shelby unique is the fact that he
is, in every sense of the word, a Legitimate Man:
real, down-to-earth and sincerely truthful about
the issues of various, numerous, complex scenarios and quagmire situations that may women go
through when dealing with the men in their lives.

However, what specifically makes Shelby so

totally unlike any other guy I have known who deals with these particular relationship issues and topics in a way that is so completely honest, sincerely caring and shooting directly from the hip is this:

"Men" who write such books—claiming to be helping women to more effectively deal with their *complicated* and complex relationship issues with men—are usually either Players or Pussy Cats.

***Players:*** There are hundreds of books out there written supposedly for *you*, from the perspective of a guy who still thinks with the mind-set and intentions of a Player. So while his grasp and understanding of the *complicated* issues at hand are probably pretty darned accurate (after all, he's exactly the guy from whom he is now supposedly trying to protect you), his true intentions are highly suspect.

Is this guy really looking to defend your virtue, heart, feelings and honor, or is he simply playing his cards to create a reputation that will draw women into his web? Is he trying to pull unsuspecting ladies like you out of one manipulative and emotionally stressful situation, only to perfectly position you to be able to easily thrust his own terrible situation into your life, if you give him just half the chance to do so?

This guy is the perfect example of the proverbial fox guarding the henhouse or the wolf in sheep's clothing. *Beware!* Remember the story of Little Red Riding-Hood and the wolf in Grandma's cozy, comfy bed: "Why, Grandma, what big, strong hands you have!"

***Pussy Cats:*** Then on the other side of the scales, you have your collection of Pussy Cats, those guys who are in every woman's life: the Best Buddy who is seemingly destined to always be your chum and pal, but never your man, boyfriend or lover.

You know the guy! He's a regular fixture in practically every Teen Dream drama, movie or TV show ever written. He's the Honorary Chick with access behind the scenes, because instead of approaching you as a man, he acts more like one of the girls. He's the guy you confide all your secrets to. He's the guy you share your inner desires with, because you know he would never have the, uh, the confidence to make his move on you himself.

Guess what, ladies? When Players and Pussy Cats write books about dealing with the deep, dark, dirty, *complicated* and complex inner-relationship scenarios between the Men and Bad Boys that you encounter in your love life, do you really think these are guys who know from experience what's really going on when things are hot and heavy, moving beyond seductively sensual to scintillatingly sizzling?

So what you frankly want is a guy who was once a powerful and successful Player, who lived the life from the exact same perspective and thought patterns as the guys with whom you are struggling to work things out today.

You want someone who was there—thinking the thoughts and doing the deeds—someone who had a Grand Awakening, an Inner Revelation, in which suddenly his human heart, mind, soul and spirit kicked into gear and, in a flash of bright light, discovered the dark and trivial emptiness in being a Dawg!

It's quite often these powerful experiences at the bottom of the barrel that position us to abruptly awaken to the reality that there simply has to be something so much truer, deeper, more real, respectable, meaningful, personally satisfying and long-lasting than these pointless, shallow, physical flings with a ridiculously long line of two-dimensional, cartoon-cutout women.

This is the tour guide who intimately knows the territory like the back of his own hand, because he once lived it as his own life for so long. But now he has seen the light and now rededicated his life to helping women just like you to learn how to safely and securely avoid all of the dangerous snakes, traps, cliffs, pitfalls, quicksand, lions, tigers and bears (oh my) that you could unwittingly run into out there in the jungle if you aren't careful and completely prepared for what's waiting for you!

So ladies, without any further ado, I present to you your own personal Player Reborn, who has arrived with the answers you seek and the solutions you need to survive this crazy little thing called *love*. Your private, personal limousine has arrived and is ready to offer you that much-needed Ride to the Other Side.

Are you ready to face reality and begin the

journey to your own personal happiness, satisfaction and joy, to be a part of a legitimate relationship that will provide you with pleasure, comfort, fun, excitement and those occasional moments when the energy of Man + Woman = A Touch of Bliss stemming from that Eternal Flame, to experience the warmth and the heat, without getting burned or being consumed?

Then let the adventure begin! Remember, the truest possible value of the entire expedition is often as much about the journey itself as it is about the eventual arrival at your chosen destination! The most meaningful experiences will be those occurring inside of you, not all around you.

With that, I bid you, *"Bon voyage!"*

Larry L. Nichols

*Larry L. Nichols is a writer of 30 years' experience who has successfully served the writing needs of his loyal, valued clients, from major world-class celebrities and Fortune 50 corporations to startup entrepreneurs with a sincere and deep passion, vision and mission: to manifest Dreams into Tangible Realities.*

On Words and Up Words!
*http://www.wordandwebwiz.com*
*http://www.larrylnichols.wordpress.com*
*"Words are my paints—minds are my canvases."*

# introduction

*L*adies, the fact is that you've been struggling far too long, constantly dealing
with *complicated* situations and relationship scenarios that have kept you from achieving
the true, deep, life-enhancing happiness, comfort,
safety, satisfaction and bliss in life that you so very
much desire and deserve to enjoy.

Achieving ultimate relationship success and
happiness—that seemingly illusory treasure you
so very much want—isn't at all what one might
call a selfish or self-centered goal or motive. So
the very first thing you need to do is get that judg-
mental, self-destructive idea and attitude out of
your head right away.

However, you are very perceptive and insightful if you pick up on the reality that your optimum
accomplishments in this pursuit of true, relational
bliss with your man, have absolutely everything to
do with *self*!

I do not mean *self* as in putting yourself first or

your own selfish needs above those of others. For this process to work effectively, you will need to be completely willing to look deeply into your inner self and be honest about what you find. You may need to change, tweak, fine-tune—or possibly just throw it out and start from scratch—if you are going to be authentically and legitimately happy and satisfied.

I have intentionally written this book in such a way that it is more about specific solutions and success strategies. None of our time together will be wasted dealing with theories, hypothesizing or academic gibberish that often tend to accomplish nothing more than making real, exciting life suddenly seem like a boring classroom or research laboratory.

For those of you wondering where the information provided in this book is coming from, the truth is that it's coming from the confessions, thoughts, desires, secrets, dreams, wishes, explanations and excuses that I have had numerous years to both personally and professionally discover. I have designed and developed failsafe tips and "step by simple step" strategies to successfully resolve the destructive collection of *complicated* situations that serve to make the lives of most women absolute Hell on Earth.

The information shared comes from a wide range of valuable and reliable sources, including my own personal and professional observations and experiences, as well as those of numerous friends, associates, clients and interviewees male and female.

I invested significant time in the extensive research, study, interviews and conversations needed to make this book—and your hopes for developing strong, powerful and satisfying relationships—possible.

I am writing about information revealed to me by literally hundreds of women, many just like you: looking for love (sometimes in all the wrong places) and trying to find it in what quite often must seem like a cold, cruel, calculating, careless world.

Then there are the contributions made by a wide variety of men: guys from virtually every walk of life, age, position, attitude, size, personality and character quality out there. They range from the really cool, nice guys to the extremely mean-spirited, animalistic, thoughtless, heartless, loveless jerks to whom so many women find themselves subconsciously—and sometimes, not so subconsciously—attracted.

First of all, understand there this is no betrayal of trust or loyalty in inviting the Bad Boys to the party, because after all, they are exactly the men who have the answers that you are looking for in life: *why, how, why, when, why, who, why, what, why, where, why*…and did I mention *why*?

That's precisely what you want to fully know, understand and eventually prepare yourself for—and hopefully eventually wean yourself away from—right? So if the Bad Boys aren't allowed access to the conversation, then we would be missing out on some important information, facts and stark, blunt realities that you will need to grasp and deal with if you are ever going to learn how to wrestle with these *complicated* situations and scenarios with men.

So, are you ready to get started?

# table of contents

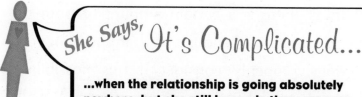

# She Says, It's Complicated...

**...when the relationship is going absolutely nowhere, but she still hangs in there anyway.**

**From Sonia in Seattle, WA**

We've been dating and living together for 7 years. I "think" that I know he loves me, but anytime I've mentioned a formal commitment, it's caused a lot of tension between us. I don't feel like it's going to amount to anything more than what it is right now, in terms of any sort of stable, long-term relationship, especially something as solid as marriage.

I was once told by a well-intentioned relationship expert that, in the minds of many women looking to experience something better in the relationship with the guy they are currently struggling with, *hope* is often little more than a delusional symptom of denial that allows the heart to keep seeking what it wants without giving up and sinking into depression or cynicism.

I think there is a certain amount of truth to that concept, at least enough truth in there for you to seriously, openly consider if this possibility might apply to you and life with your lover. We all recognize the fact that The Heart Wants What the Heart Wants, but in order to be fair to ourselves and protect our hearts, we need to honestly and clearly evaluate whether this *hope* we're living for is legitimately a strong possibility, or little more than a cold, hard pipe-dream.

Ladies, you are not helping or protecting yourselves by hiding away in a self-constructed, comfy, cozy Castle of Clouds built high in the sky, or shrouded away in a mansion of myth, mystery and a maniacal maze of manipulative mirrors that prevent you from seeing what's actually taking place right before your very eyes.

So while *hope* and *belief* can be very powerful tools in many of life's events, allowing false hopes and misguided beliefs to prevent you from fully experiencing reality as it is—keeping you from living in the moment while valuable weeks, months, years and potentially decades slip by and are lost to you forever—is actually a common form of self-sabotage.

The truth is that we all have an insightful inner voice that is deep within us, specifically placed there for precisely such a time as this. If you can allow yourself to listen carefully to what that small, quiet voice is telling you, you will always know without any shadow of a doubt what the *truth* is.

The trick is to learn how to hear what your inner voice is actually trying to tell you. That means getting out of the crazed and concerned hustle and bustle of your daily, typical life and going off by yourself into a nice, peaceful and quiet environment to decompress and get back in touch with what's really going on deep inside yourself.

The fact is, deep down inside, you honestly already know the truth—but just like Jack Nicholson's character in the film *A Few Good Men*, your conscious mind is afraid that "you can't handle the truth." As a result, you continue to allow the endless, repetitive, looping messages that *everything is going to be fine* to play throughout your conscious mind, hoping to lessen your fears and calm your concerns.

You know what? It's true that everything *is* going to be okay, but only when you turn off the illusion, ignore the false messages composed of insecurity and denial, and actually clear the stuff that isn't working for you out of your life forever. *Just let it go.*

One of those messy, destructive items that needs to be cleaned up and cleared out of your life could be the dead relationship that clearly isn't happy, healthy, working for you or going anywhere.

The good news is that when you finally take out the garbage and clean up that huge mess where your heart used to be, you will suddenly have a nice, clean, shiny, attractive space in your life that will be clear and available to the man who is authentically good for you: the constantly sought-out but rarely found Mr. Right.

The sad thing is that the reason most women never find Mr. Right is because they are so busy struggling desperately to hold onto and control Mr. Wrong that they never have the necessary free time or open consciousness to even notice Mr.

Right is *there*, and to invest the interest and energy into connecting with him when he arrives.

How unfortunate to think that the effort to do everything in your power to forcefully keep a disastrously dead and dying relationship in your life is precisely the misguided roadblock preventing a potentially perfectly fitting, wonderful relationship from blooming in your life. All of your available attention and energy are being wasted tenaciously clinging to the wrong man!

That wrong man is taking up the space that Mr. Right would naturally slide into, but he can't connect. His place is being taken up and held by a guy who doesn't even want to be there—and deep down inside, you *know* you could and should be doing better. *Ouch!*

You see, it has only become *complicated* because you have chosen to block out the natural, inherent contact that you have with your true inner self and the instincts that are telling you that this current relationship is bad news—that you deserve more than this!

It's time to leave and get on with your life, because we both know that he isn't going to change.

*Why?* The truth is that you actually *never* can change others; people only change when they decide for themselves that they want to change.

You may be able to talk him into claiming that he is going to change, but he won't—because he actually doesn't want to. He doesn't want *you*! You simply don't have the power to change anyone against his will. That's actually a good thing, or we all would be in continual risk of being manipulated and controlled against our will. What sort of a terrible life of kidnapping and slavery would that be?

So what do you have the ability to effectively change? You can only change *yourself* and what it is that you choose to do with yourself; and that includes your horrible, soul-numbing, heartbreaking relationship.

 ***Simple Solution***

It's time to bail out and move on to a guy who really wants to be with you, share with you and find happiness with and *in* you. Stop making it hard on yourself—simply take the time to look with honest, open eyes and heart at the history of your relationship with this guy. What's so different from the first few weeks and the first few months of your new, exciting and budding relationship compared to how things are going now? The answer is, "Probably nothing."

What are the clear, obvious, observable and perceptible intentions and attitudes that he is consistently demonstrating toward *you* and *your relationship*?

If it's not something exciting any more and clearly not what you want for yourself, then you need to wake up, smell the coffee and get out of this stagnant tomb of a relationship.

A wise person once told me that when people take the time to show you Who They Are, pay very careful attention to what they reveal about themselves. It's time to calmly break away positively, peacefully, amicably—but *definitely*. There's no need to have a big blowup. Just let him know that you recognize your relationship just isn't going anywhere and that this isn't good for either of you!

It's that simple. Most likely, he already knows it as well or, if not, it will prove to be a helpful, friendly wake-up call for him to start making some serious evaluations and changes in his own life to get his act together and discover what he wants out of life for himself.

The funny thing is that the only possible way to help this guy to eventually become someone worthy of a relationship is for you to move and completely clear him out of your life. So if you're still thinking that there's possibly a chance he could eventually become Mr. Right, the only way to find out is to set him free and allow him the space to be who he truly is.

So, for all of you ladies who are hoping that Mr. Wrong might learn to become Mr. Right, the fact is that as long as you try to hold onto him, he'll never have the space or opportunities to grow, and it will never happen. If you let him go and move on, then in that miraculous one-out-of-a-billion chance that it's destiny, he'll eventually walk back into your life. However, don't waste your time holding your breath, because you are far more likely to be hit twice by lightning in the same spot than experience the "frog to Prince Charming" fairy-tale ending.

***Shelby Says:***

My dear, it's time to *grow up, wake up and move on*!

# She Says, *It's Complicated...*

**...when he cheats on her and she continues to stay with him.**

**From Barbara in Atlanta, GA**

*He's cheated on me twice. I know I should leave him, but I love him. He says it won't happen again. I'm so torn and confused.*

**H**ey, I'll be the first to tell you that being cheated on by someone you love is not a peaceful walk on the beach with the sun shimmering off the ocean carrying a light breeze that softly caresses your face. It feels more like your heart has been snatched out of your body and your soul is sinking helplessly into a pit of flaming quicksand. Luckily for me, that woman is not my current loving and faithful wife.

Questions constantly pound in your head as you continue to hear the chaotic chorus of a million off-key, out-of-tune, distressed voices crying out in desperation, *Why? Why? Why?* What's even worse is the fact that when you begin to regain consciousness and a moderate semblance of sanity, you realize that the entire frightening chorus howling inside of your mind is actually *you. How could he do this to me?* You were so very certain that he really loved you, and you most certainly were happily and actively loving him with all of your heart, body, mind and soul. So how could this happen to *you?*

Does that sound familiar? At least now you can tell from my words that you aren't alone and that I know from personal experience exactly what you are going through. Oh sure, when you first get cheated on, the shock momentarily deludes and confuses you into believing that your situation is uniquely different, one of a kind, first time ever—and nobody else out there can possibly understand what you are going through.

But trust me, I know. That's just your shaken and shocked mind reacting to the sudden grief and anguish talking "nonsense" to you. You are hoping to figure out a way to possibly protect yourself from the pain and suffering of stark reality.

The truth is that even though every snowflake or fingerprint is different, there are a number of verified, general truths about snow and fingers proved by scientists that we can all agree upon. In the very same way, relationships also are unique to the two particular individuals involved, yet there are some general principles and truths that apply to all relationships.

So while the idea of your man's cheating on you might temporarily seem to be the biggest catastrophe in human history right now, the sooner you come to clearly understand that there are some basic, consistent, reliable, tried, tested, and true generalities that can help get you though this situation, the better off you're going to be.

Here's the thing: he's cheated and you have for some reason decided to stay with him. This is a decision that *you* made. Unfortunately, in today's oversexed society of promiscuity and lavish, lusty lasciviousness, the common street perception is that in today's world, people cheat all the time—so you may as well just get used to it, expect it and accept it.

But do *you* honestly agree with that? Is that what your personal love life has come to now—just accepting the unacceptable and trying to ignore the reality of what the event is trying to teach you?

Cheating is merely the symptom of something far more seriously wrong festering below the perceptible surface. Cheating is a problem, but it isn't *the* problem—and until you courageously and honestly face the real problem, you will continue to experience a long and consistent line of similar problems.

Is that what your life has come to? Or do you deserve something better, deeper, more noble, true and special than a love life sullied and spoiled by infidelity, deceit and disrespect?

People cheat for various reasons. It's *complicated* when you decide to try and stick it out with a cheater to work things out with him, because as is often the case, cheating says more about the character of the cheater than it does about you and your relationship.

That means that as hard as you may try to make everything at home perfect, that flaw in character is not being addressed and will more than likely raise its ugly, destructive head again and again. Can you get your mind around that truth and come to terms with the implications that it brings to your life?

Perhaps it was a one-time mistake, and the cheater is truly sorry, repentant and willing to do whatever it takes to save the relationship. That is a possibility, though the odds are that those are more the words of either well-meaning best intentions or cleverly worded deceit intended to soften your anger and shock to sway your consciousness back to sleep so that the cheating can resume.

 **Simple Solution**

Honestly, of all the solutions written in this book, this one may be the least simple and clear, because there actually are occasions of one-time slip-ups that strike unexpectedly when he was vulnerable and unprepared to deal with the temptation. Maybe he really is sorry, sincerely seeks your forgiveness and wants to save the relationship.

Most of the time, *repetitive* evidence will come to prove that that is not the case—but let's say we are going to give the guy the benefit of the doubt.

Okay, then you need to have a strong, deep, revealing and heart-felt "soul to soul" conversation that seeks out what hidden issues are lurking in the darkness and bring them kicking and screaming out into the bright light of day.

You *need to know* in no uncertain terms exactly what's going on and why this happened in order to prevent its recurrence. If you don't get to the factual heart and source of the matter, it is definitely going to keep recurring.

Also there have to be some strict boundaries set up, along with some clearly, precisely defined penalties that will be applied to the fullest extent of the law's provisions should either one of you stray from the agreed-upon rules of conduct. That means, in some situations, it is actually the actions, attitudes, comments or lack of them that will make a man feel as if he is not or no longer respected, loved, or needed.

All that needs to be thoroughly cleared up and discussed in full—and then a set of unbendable, non-negotiable rules needs to be put in place to help ensure that these certain scenarios now known to set things off never occur again.

By the way, one condition that needs to be strictly adhered to is the rule about cheating itself, as in, "If you do that one more time, I'm definitely kicking your sorry butt to the curb and moving on, buddy, so you'd better watch yourself and your actions most carefully."

 *Shelby Says:*

Hey, I'm a man, and for the most part, I believe people deserve a second chance. I don't necessarily subscribe to the "he cheated once, he'll do it again" philosophy. However, if he's done it twice, you most definitely should *beat it*.

# She Says, It's Complicated...

**...when she's in love with him, but he's married.**

**From Denise in Akron, OH**

I've been seeing a man for 4 months now. When we met, it was on a business trip and we instantly hit it off right away.

Yes...he was wearing a wedding ring and at first, I thought we might "just be friends," but he quickly opened up and shared with me that he was very unhappy and had already made up his mind that he was going to leave his wife when he returned home from this trip.

Wow, the timing couldn't have been more perfect had this chance meeting actually been planned for!

Anyway, like I said, it's been 4, almost 5 months now and he still hasn't left her, or for all I know, even broached the subject with her.

Due to the nature of our professions, it's

relatively easy for us to see each other fairly frequently, even though we live in different states.

OK, here's the thing. Now I've basically fallen in love with the guy, but it's becoming more and more clear to me that he actually still loves his wife and seems to be pretty comfortable with the situation "as is!"

This being the case, there obviously isn't any real chance of any sort of a future for "US!"

Boy, do I feel like I got suckered into this one! What now?!

Face it: what could possibly be more *complicated* than a relationship in which one of you is married and the other one isn't? First of all, it means that the entire relationship is built on the foundation of deceit and thoughtlessly being willing to hurt—or even destroy—another person's life, happiness, sense of security, marriage and family.

Those are some pretty hefty negative building blocks to base any relationship on, especially for *you* if he is the one who is married. You see, this type of lopsided arrangement quite automatically, unfairly and severely sways the degree of personal control and risk that each of you experiences in the situation.

Honestly, you have to ask yourself, *If his wife and possibly kids, obviously have no logical reason to trust in and rely on him, why should I be willing to do so when I actually already know beyond any shadow of a doubt that he is a cheater? So what in the world would stop him from cheating on* me?

Relationships that work are based on creating environments in which both of you can feel free to let your guard down and allow yourself to feel at ease, comfortable, safe, vulnerable and open to connecting at the very deepest human levels, with sincerity and authenticity!

What are the chances that his being married to another woman on whom he is currently cheating with *you* could in some way eventually, negatively affect your relationship in a destructive and painful manner?

So yeah, it's *complicated* when he's married and you're not. Actually, all affaires that involve a married partner are *complicated*, but that's a whole other story. For now, let's simply focus on your particular situation.

Alright, so now you find yourself in love with a married man and he appears to be showing no signs of clearing out the wife to make room for the two of you to be together as planned. *Ouch!*

These are the dangers to which you can very quickly and easily fall prey when you don't go into Dating Mode with some already predetermined rules, principles and policies worked out in advance—and absolutely committed to.

Love and lust both have a strong, seductive pulling power, and if you don't decide well ahead of time how you are going to respond to certain situations, you may be perilously drawn in before you are even able to gauge exactly what's happening to you.

Let me guess: you were just out for a little fun to blow off some steam after a long day of business-as-usual. He was pretty hot and looked like he was loving what he saw in you. So what's the harm in a little semi-erotic dance of flirtation and fun, correct?

You were probably thinking that since he's

clearly married, he's not going to take this seriously, and so he's safe to toy around with for a night, right?

Maybe it was Happy Hour, you both had a bit too much to drink and then suddenly the chemistry started flowing incredibly strongly between the two of you. It was simply way too good to just walk away from without seeing exactly what was going on there, so you decided, at least momentarily, to ignore all of the warning signs and proceed with the conversation.

However, a simple conversation quickly turned into way more than you had originally planned or bargained for. Before you knew what was happening, sparks were flying, energy was being generated and there was No Way Out—or at least so it seemed under the influence of alcohol and excited passions.

Okay, you can't go back and change what's already happened, so rather than beat yourself up over ancient history, let's find your way out of the maze.

First of all, you need to fully understand the following *typical situations* that you are *nearly always* going to encounter when attempting to be in any sort of relationship with a married man:

### *He's married...*
### *but claims he's unhappy or leaving her.*

This tends to be The Safest Play for most married guys looking to score a little on the side, because you can't ever get mad at him for not being completely up front and totally honest with you, disclosing from Moment One that he's a married man.

This, Denise, is where you are finding yourself caught right now with your current *complicated* situation. You see, I'm not saying this guy intended to be a Player, but most Dawgs know that this scenario is the safest play for them to get away with having their cake at home and eating a little on the side when they're out to play.

He admits from the beginning that he is married but unhappy. This sets him up as the Good Guy, the poor, innocent victim here. He loves his wife and wants to make it work, but she or life just isn't cooperating with poor, brokenhearted, sad, innocent Hubby.

A great way for you to avoid such sticky circumstances in the future is to ask him a very simple question. "What exactly do you. mean by 'unhappy?'"

Asking this will help you begin to unravel what's really going on at the heart of the situation and position you to ask even more direct questions that will help you to dig down to the very roots of what's up and what his hidden intentions are—hooking up with you.

If you really want to see a married man squirm, simply ask him two or more very direct-and-to-the-point questions about his marriage. You'll most likely see him desperately reach for a fictional reply. Once he knows more questions are coming, he'll sprint out of your sight faster than the rocket he was just aiming at you only moments before.

### He's married...
### but he's separated.

This one is a bit trickier. You see, married-but-separated men still view this position as effectively and honestly covering their proverbial tracks with full disclosure that they're married. Yet it also leaves them a lot of wiggle room and a very convenient emergency escape route should they ever decide that they need to use the Salvaging My Marriage and Going Back to My Wife backup safety net to bail out on you.

In other words, the two of you may have a little physical fun but if you begin to start looking for some sort of an emotional connection, the odds are he will be out of there in no time flat.

He may choose to take the Semi-High School Road and try to considerately let you down softly by explaining that his wife and he have decided to reconcile and try to work things out.

Or he can just completely and suddenly disappear from your radar entirely without a single word of explanation, assuming that you knew he was married all along—so you knew what you were getting yourself into from the very beginning.

Either way, for your own protection and sanity, if you come into contact with a married guy who says he's separated and he seems interested in you, turn right around and run like hell in the opposite direction. *You have been warned!*

### He's married ...
### but doesn't tell you until you've slept
### together...perhaps several times.

These guys are by far, the very the worst. This is the kind of man who gently and affectionately kisses his cookie-cutter wife as he walks out the door, drives away from his cookie-cutter home in their cookie-cutter neighborhood—supposedly off to play poker with the boys—but actually heads to the local club or bar to meet *you*!

Sadly, you are nothing more than a temporary respite from what he perceives as mundane monotony, where he can enjoy the momentary excitement of getting his ego and other unmentionable parts stroked.

There are a million cute and willing distractions from his everyday routine, and he is hoping that tonight the mini-vacation will be you. So he quite casually and confidently slips off his wedding ring before entering the bar scene and ensures that he is specially groomed to look as single as possible.

To you, he may look like the ultimate bachelor: clean-cut, well-dressed, cool, calm and collected—and perhaps a bit cocky—well established and financially stable. He's your knight in shining armor.

No wonder it's so easy for this particular guy to be incredibly confident: after all, if he's properly prepared for tonight's conquest, he pretty much has everything to gain and believes that if he picks precisely the right type of woman, he has relatively little chance of losing anything in the encounter.

So when he meets you, he says all of the right things and demonstrates all of the right moves. You're thinking, *Wow...chivalry isn't dead after all! This is exactly how I've always wanted to be treated by a guy.*

And, of course, he knows it—because that was all part of his diabolical plan from the very beginning.

Here's what you can look for and receive— guaranteed. About half-way into your evening together (once he feels relatively assured that things are moving along in The Right Direction and that he is most likely going to score what he actually came for), he'll mention that he has a big business meeting or an important flight to catch early in the morning, so he won't be able to spend the night with you.

Next, prepare to be buttered up one side and down the other with comments about how he can't believe he has met such a totally awesome woman, so incredibly beautiful, smart, deep, caring and fun to be with.

He's hoping that you'll be so totally blown away by his positive assessment and appreciation of *you* that you won't want to risk possibly missing out on finding Mr. Right, so you'll decide to expedite your connection...and by that, of course, I mean physical connection.

So maybe you actually end up sleeping with him on the first night, or maybe you manage to hold onto your virtue and choose not to. The point is that this game has only two possible outcomes: (1) either you sleep with him—soon—or (2) he will suddenly be informed that he is being called to move back to the corporate office 1,000 miles away.

If you *do* end up sleeping with him, human emotions will do what they were naturally designed to do, and you will end up falling for the guy. You can disagree right now, but it's simply inevitable; if we talk in a month or so, you'll be singing a different tune.

Predictably, every time you see him, he won't be able to stay all night or for too long. The trick is that his job is to sell himself to you and always leave you desperately wanting more and more of him. Meanwhile, he's got his cookie-cutter wife to whom he needs to return at his palace in Candy Land!

Once you've finally fallen in love—and you will—you'll begin to want, desire and eventually demand more. That is precisely where the mythological Golden Egg begins to crack and get messy.

Prepare yourself: expect to hear the following response—or something very much along the same line. "Hey, I'm really sorry, but I'm married. I didn't expect to fall for you this way, but I can't continue to do this anymore; it's not fair to either of us or my wife."

While it's true that you will *still* most likely end up being desperately disappointed and deeply hurt, at least you won't be so totally surprised or completely confused by the situation and unable to surmise exactly what's happening to you.

Okay, so what the hell are you supposed to do now? At this stage you very well may have already invested months into this relationship, and it's not exactly easy to just turn around and walk away.

### *Simple Solution*

Plain and simple: as soon as you find out that the guy is married, a Red Flag of Warning should instantly be going up inside your mind, heart and soul!

Regardless of his proclamations of true love for you—despite his promises to leave his wife for you, and no matter how hard and long he tries to convince you that he is so deeply and desperately unhappy with his marriage and is already in the process of getting out of it—protect your heart, soul, mind and virtue, and get out of there and away from him as fast as you can and never look back.

I understand that *right now,* you sincerely feel

like you love him—as would any women in your situation having just experienced all that you have with him. It's natural; and believe me, you're not the first or last woman to go through this nightmare.

There are plenty of other women who have been down this road before, and I have coached them into successfully coming out on the other side—not only surviving but thriving! In fact, they are happier than ever because of the experience. Had they not succumbed to the Married Guy, they might never have realized how to avoid similar *complicated* situations in the future.

This is most certainly *not* saying that, just knowing this information in advance, you would never intentionally allow yourself to fall into this quagmire because it would be thoroughly self-destructive. However, it is good to know that like every great lesson in life, you often have to make some mistakes to truly learn what's what—and that is especially so in relationships!

It's natural for you to question whether he truly ever loved you and why he did all of this if he truly loves his wife. The more and more you continue to think about it, the more all of those unanswered questions pound in your head.

As you open that Pandora's Box, more and more questions will continue to arise, all of which will seem absolutely vital for him to answer if you are ever to be able to fully recover and move on.

Trust me, that sort of obsessive thinking is nothing more than a trap, and you have already wasted too much of your valuable time on a guy who has now proved beyond the shadow of a doubt to be not worth another moment of your precious time.

In fact, the more you actually get to know about the guy, the bigger the disappointment— not only in him for being such a jerk, but in yourself for being so very naïve as to fall for this charlatan's charade.

Every woman whom I have ever interviewed, who pushed the issue and insisted on getting some answers, was always left feeling more hurt and betrayed as the man would either refuse to talk to her or simply because the answers that she got weren't anything at all like what she was hoping to hear.

Here's the only answer you need: true love may very well be waiting for you just around the corner, but you'll never be ready, willing or able to experience it as long as you are emotionally wrapped up in the disaster that you just experienced with this loser.

So save some face and dignity, pick yourself up, brush yourself off and move on to where true love can find you at last.

 *Shelby Says:*

Girl, you really need to get rid of that notion that he's ever actually going to leave his wife for you. All the empirical data on such situations show that 98.9% of the time, it just doesn't happen.

It's time to face the facts, my friend. The truth is that you served one purpose and one purpose only with this guy—you were a momentary escape from what he perceives as the monotony of monogamy!

If you think you can rein him in and somehow magically rekindle your flame by pitching a tantrum and making either veiled or direct threats, trust me: he'll drop you faster than you can finish reading this sente...

## She Says, It's Complicated...

**...when the sex is incredible, but he won't commit to a relationship.**

### From Jamie in Greenville, NC

I'm just going to get right to the point. We have sex every chance we get. I like it, in fact, I love it. Thing is, I know that's all that there is and probably will always be between us.

I keep telling myself that it takes time to develop a relationship, but now I'm starting to worry that no matter how much time I give him to see how great we are together, he's probably never going to come around for anything more than the sex.

t's *complicated* because *sex* is what I call Mortal Kryptonite for us humans. Yes indeed! At first sex may seem to be a pleasure that affects us purely on a physical level, but before we know it, it has a mysterious, almost mystical, way of somehow sneaking into other aspects of our mind, heart and soul.

Particularly into our subconscious minds, where if we aren't careful—and usually most of us aren't—it can begin to cause all sorts of unexpected havoc and complex, *complicated* situations for ourselves as well as others.

Sex is an extremely powerful energy and experience that can unexpectedly get in there and begin to cause us to lose accurate measure of our values as people and to seductively draw us toward irrational thoughts, decisions, points of view and compromises that under normal circumstances we would never dream of making.

Sex can also take an extremely dramatic toll on us, causing us to say and do things that we have strongly vowed all ourlives we would *never ever* say or do. Anyone who tells you differently is either lying, deeply deceived, in total denial or a virgin!

Sex can drain a soul and weaken the will of just about anybody—regarding just about anything—especially when it's really, really Great Sex and the person who suddenly holds the keys to whether you get it or not is someone who you find uncontrollably attractive.

Okay, look, it's a completely normal experience in life—both biologically and psychologically—that when you're having absolutely explosive, mind-blowing sex with a guy, you're simply going to eventually get completely lost in him and what it is that he does *to* you and *for* you.

In other words, it's normal that, when you connect with a partner who provides heart-pounding, toe-clenching sex, you are naturally going to begin, at least temporarily, to totally lose yourself in the awesome wonder of the experience and, therefore, in Mr. X as well.

Now here's a fact that you really need to get your mind around and understand like the gospel truth: men already *know* this fact and they know it well! Guys realize that they don't have to be the most handsome, wealthy, stable, reliable, considerate man—or even the biggest stud in the herd—in order to get you wrapped around his, well, you know. All he needs is to know how to push your buttons and make you cry out for more.

Most men put a lot of pride into their ability to sexually please a woman. This is because in a world that culturally gives women the control to decide whether or not sex is going to happen, his mastery of the craft of making you hot suddenly turns the tables and gives him the upper hand.

 ***Warning!***

Most men are extremely capable and quite adept at completely separating what feels good to them from their emotions. Most of these guys have the ability and common tendency to simply indulge in the physical sensations of getting laid, quickly losing interest and moving on to their next item on the agenda—as if intercourse with you was nothing more than a quick meal at a fast-food joint.

Most women however, aren't like that and aren't prepared to deal with so very suddenly being dismissed by a man who only 15 minutes ago was telling her that she is The Most Beautiful and Uniquely Special Lady on Earth. This is a big part of the epic, age-old Battle of the Sexes that women just don't seem to fully understand.

Many of you have tried and usually just as

many have failed. This is because women tend to tie emotion in with sex. They usually feel very vulnerable when lying there in bed, naked and climaxing repeatedly. This man who is working his magic suddenly seems to be some sort of a god or heroic figure in his abiity to make her feel such powerful sensations. And with women, along with these sensations come emotions.

She begins to sort it all out in her head: *Wow, he really must love me to take care of me so carefully, intimately, precisely. Obviously, he's chosen to be with me over all the other women around. He must really have a strong thing for me, this is so wonderfully awesome. I am special!*

Sorry to wake you from your dream, my dear, but yes, he most certainly does have a Strong Thing for you. Sadly though, in reality, he would be just as happy sharing his strong thing with a million other women out there. In his genetic makeup, he thinks he is being a really giving prince by seriously considering coming back to *you* and allowing you to enjoy "seconds."

It's just a matter of the gigantic differences in how men and women are wired genetically and programmed culturally. Of course, not every single guy out there is a thoughtlessly raging hormone looking for a female to explode in, just as not every woman is an emotional, nesting lover looking to build a permanent future with the first guy who can make her squirm or scream for that matter.

These are just strong, well-founded biological tendencies that we all need to keep in mind in order to effectively and safely understand the rules and strategies in this crazy little game called *sex*.

So here are the facts: you have a guy who consistently seeks you out and the two of you have absolutely awesome sex together. So far, that's 100% accurate and completely true.

Now you start to assume that because he returns to you again and again to make you feel so totally, wonderfully womanly, that he's progressively falling more and more in love with you and that he's definitely a long-term relationship Keeper.

*Ding, ding, ding!* That bell is a warning that you have just stepped out of reality and are now floating aimlessly in an abyss located somewhere between delusion and denial.

These sorts of vulnerable thoughts, feelings and assumptions are precisely what open you up wide enough to fall victim to a very long and seemingly endless line of disappointment, pain and frustration. If you keep thinking like that, he's got you right where he wants you.

Your feminine nature and nurture are telling you that because the two of you are having great sex, then you obviously must be in a relationship—but that's not exactly true. Remember: according to his masculine genetics and psychology, sex does not necessarily equal relationship in the mind of a man.

If the two of you are having great sex, then trust me, he doesn't want to lose this highly enjoyable synergistic experience with you either. But if he begins to feel like there are strings or conditions attached, he is very likely going to feel like he needs to run for his life.

So, in order to protect yourself from getting hurt, keep this in mind: if he's not ready to show some truly clear signs of beginning to commit after two to three months of dating, don't set yourself up for pain and anguish by expecting anything more than what you're already getting. As long as you're still enjoying it, it may be perfectly fine—as long as you are being honest with yourself.

 **Simple Solution**

You need to take a break from all of this and make some time to clear your head and heart. Simply get a hold of yourself. There is much more to a real, legitimate relationship than just great sex. You know this deep down inside, which is why you are already feeling uncomfortable and frustrated.

Get your mind out of the clouds and your feet back on the ground. At least, temporarily step back from the situation, because you need to come to an understanding that while it may be totally mind-bending sex, that's *all* it is and nothing more.

Make a list and write down everything that the two of you have in common. I don't mean little things like your favorite ice cream flavor or sports

team. I mean significant values, interests, joys, beliefs, views, dreams, visions and plans for the future. What truly important key commonalities do
the two of you share?

Here's a helpful hint: if you don't even *know*
what his values, interests, joys, beliefs, views,
dreams, visions and plans for the future are, then
this is *not* a relationship—it's just great sex.

By the way, I'm assuming that you are interested enough in your own life to definitely know for
yourself what *your* significant values, interests,
joys, beliefs, views, dreams, visions and plans for
the future are. If not, stop wasting your time
thinking about who you want to settle down with
and start directing that energy into who, where,
what, why and when *you* want to be in life.

If you discover that you actually do have some
significant keys in common, then what are his
goals for the next two, three and five years—and
do they fit or coincide with yours? What are his
life objectives and aspirations? Are they in line and
tracking with yours?

Does he want a wife and family and, if so,
when? Maybe he's already had that and doesn't

desire it anymore, or at least for a long time. These types of key questions will give you a very clear picture of exactly what the two of you do or don't have in common.

What you are most likely going to discover from this exercise is that it confirms what you have been feeling all along: that your lives are not in sync and heading in the same direction, but rather it's just really good sex. Good to know, don't you think?

Simply getting yourself these vital, life-saving answers to those significant key questions makes it all that much easier to break away from the kryptonite. The mesmerizing mystery of the sex begins to lose its power, because in the stark light of day it can clearly be seen as something fundamentally flawed and utterly empty.

 *Shelby Says:*

Hey, it's just a sex thing! What is it that you don't understand?

## She Says, *It's Complicated...*

**...when she wants to break up, but she can't because of finances.**

**From Daisy in Killeen, TX**

Please help me. I don't know what to do, but I've got to do something, and fast! He's the breadwinner, there's no question about that. He makes a good living but that's not enough for me anymore.

He's controlling and demanding and I know that if I try to leave him, he's not going to support me in any way. We've been together for 7 years but we aren't married.

What should I do?

sn't it interesting how money somehow manages to have a hand in just about everything we do? We can't go on vacation or even a nice date unless we have money. You constantly hear all sorts of stories about people who can't get married unless they have money—and now apparently some people can't even break up a bad relationship, because they don't have money.

These are the sorts of things I hear from women all the time: "He takes care of all of the bills." "He makes the larger salary." "I can't afford to live on my own." "I don't have job." "I can't pay the bills with my salary alone." "I've never had to work before." "I'd love to get a job, but wouldn't know where to start."

Hey, I don't mean to sound cruel or cliché here, but the bottom line is: *if you have the will, then you will find—or more importantly make—the way.*

Does it really make sense to stay in an unhappy, unfulfilling, cold and lonely relationship with a man who you really don't want to be with emotionally or physically? Should money be the major factor involved in deciding who you are going to spend your life with?

I'm going to give you the benefit of the doubt and assume your answer to my questions is a resounding, "No!" Okay then! I totally understand that the lack of money can make things a bit *complicated*, but they are by no means anywhere even close to being insurmountable. As long as you are truly and sincerely serious about improving your circumstances, nothing is impossible.

You simply have to begin to value yourself and your happiness above mere money and realize that money is nothing more than a convenient tool created out of paper and metal, allowing people to exchange buying power with one another. So ask yourself this: *Am I more important than a pile of paper and metal?*

 **Simple Solution**

I want you to think back to a time in your life when you had the goal to buy something that you really, really wanted. As it turned out, it was pretty darned expensive and financially out of your reach. Or perhaps there was a time when you had to raise a certain amount of money for some special event, like a trip, charity or fundraiser.

Can you remember all the way back to your childhood, when you wanted your very first bike or makeup kit, or maybe you wanted to win the Grand Prize for selling the most Girl Scout cookies? Just close your eyes for 30 seconds and think about that particular scenario.

I'm willing to bet you probably had no idea how you were going to raise the money to get what you wanted at the time. I'm also willing to bet you figured out a really simple strategy that worked perfectly to help you accomplish your financial goal. I'm further willing to bet that if you didn't fully achieve your goal, you probably came pretty darn close to it, didn't you?

The point here is that you used your inherent intelligence to figure out a way to get what you needed when you were faced with a financial deficit. You did it then, and I promise you that you can do it again—this time even better than the first time, because now you are an adult.

Too often, cultural stereotypes project the image of attractive women being stupid, ignorant, empty-headed, gold-digging, pieces of eye candy, who can't fend for themselves, so they have to have Sugar Daddies take care of them.

That's an absolute lie and a completely sad, sick and disgusting stereotype for any culture to promote about its own female population. However, what would be even more sad, sick and disgusting is for *you* to actually start to believe such nonsense about yourself!

If you know that you truly want out of the relationship—but money is tight and blocking the way to your escape—then use that smart brain of yours to creatively design and engineer your own way to achieving your objective. It's actually as simple as sitting down with a pen and paper and beginning to write down and answer some questions:

> ### My worst-case scenario:
> *Will he hurt me if I left him today?*
> *Where would I sleep if I left today?*
> *How would I eat if I left today?*
> *How will I support myself if I left today?*

OK, now it's time to write out:

> ### My best-case scenario:
> *I'll finally be FREE to live the life I've always dreamed of for myself.*
>
> *I'll finally be FREE to pursue relationships I'm truly interested in.*

Great job! That was excellent work and you must be feeling pretty excited and proud of yourself right now. So let's take advantage of the positive energy and immediately get started in a very simple, easy-to-follow, "step by simple step" process to achieving your goal.

If you don't have a job right now, what are your options for getting one? Start combing the newspaper want ads as well as asking friends, family members and neighbors whether they have any employment openings, leads or referrals they could make for you with their personal and professional contacts.

What are your current bills, including life expenses, such as a car, insurance, food budget, average utility costs, plus things like memberships, associations, along with credit cards and doctors' bills?

How much money will you need to deal with unplanned contingencies, such as your car breaking down, or replacing a burned-out TV or computer?

Okay, now how much money do you currently have in the bank?

Where else do you have money pending or available to you, for example, stocks, bonds, CDs, or a claim/settlement payment coming your way? How willing are you to tap into whatever financial resources are available to you?

What else do you have of value that you haven't yet thought of? Perhaps you have a treasure chest of expensive heirloom jewelry, or a precious book, record, magazine or china-and-silverware collection. Speaking of collections, what about stamps, coins, dolls, classic toys such as Easy-Bake Ovens, Cabbage Patch dolls or Barbies, maybe even classic lunch boxes—anything at all?

After you've answered these questions, go back to your list of "Worst Case Scenarios" and begin to re-evaluate each one of your initial concerns, fears and worries with your newfound confidence and excitement and call this list:

### My most-likely-case scenario:

For example:

*Will he hurt me if I left him today?*

Hardly likely at all; you have the law on your side and he isn't going to want to risk destroying his reputation or losing his job, friends and public standing by hurting his girlfriend, especially in a relationship that has lost its spark and is clearly dead or dying. If you're still concerned, simply take some friends and a video camera with sound along with you for protection and as witnesses of what transpires.

Odds are that you will be amazingly and positively surprised to discover nothing bad happens at all, outside of the possibility of a few hurtful words exchanged at the initial moment of contact and explanation of the situation.

Trust me, having those friends there (at least one or two guys if possible) and a video camera or two with sound, he'll quickly realize it's in his very best interest to be on his best behavior. If not, he's clearly a psychopath you need to get away from even more desperately than you originally realized.

*Where would I sleep if I left today?*

Come on now, do you really expect me to believe that you don't have a string of friends, neighbors, family and associates with whom you can temporarily crash for a while as you are putting your new life together?

If not, there are all kinds of very helpful and caring living-assistance programs set up by numerous organizations, churches and charities, as well as the city, state, county and federal programs. They are there to help specifically in your precise situation; all you have to do is ask.

*How would I eat if I left today?*

Again, I really doubt very much that your friends, family and neighbors would simply just sit back and let you starve or even go hungry for a day. People reach out to the needy all the time! It's a wonderfully inherent, instinctive part of being *human*.

When catastrophes or bad circumstances

come along, people with food, clothes and other necessities come running to the rescue—and that's for total strangers whom they've never even met before. How do you think homeless people survive on the street for years? Only through the kindness of strangers, that's how!

So I can't imagine your friends, neighbors and family turning their backs on you when you are trying to finally get your life together and stand on your own two feet. If they don't want to offer help, ask them for a loan that you will gladly pay back when you have your new job and place.

Otherwise, all of those organizations that I mentioned in the previous question are actually much more capable of helping out with things like food, clothing, and medical assistance. So no matter what, you are going to be fine.

*How will I support myself if I left today?*

Suddenly, that doesn't seem to be such a big worry any more, after going over all of your options and making some concrete plans to get it all taken care of, does it?

Wow! Congratulations: you have just taken the

steps to prepare yourself for the most exciting, satisfying, positive and fun adventure of your life. *Bon voyage*; it's going to be great!

### Shelby Says:

Question: What's more important here, money or happiness? There are two things a smart, confident woman will never have to worry about: one of them is money and the other is men.

A woman who truly has her act together will always have as much and as many of both as she needs. Remember Tina Turner? She left Ike when her best years were supposedly behind her, with nothing more than 38 cents to her name. So how did she end up doing for herself?

Cher left Sonny after the TV show was cancelled and things were looking pretty bleak. But last I heard, she's doing pretty well for herself, living a life most of us could only dream of.

Now if that's not inspirationally encouraging, I really don't know what else to tell you. You simply need to go for it and make your own special dreams come true—for yourself and by yourself. You can definitely do it; all you have to do is try.

Don't wait until you finally, truly believe that you can do it before you start the process. Instead, simply allow the effects of your efforts themselves to then automatically create the positive outcomes that will—over a short period of time—give you the indisputable proof needed to be convinced that you truly *believe*!

Go for it!

She Says, It's Complicated...

...when she doesn't love him, but she likes having him around.

**From Mary in Reno, NV**

Listen, I kind of like him. I think he's a really nice guy but I don't love him or anything and honestly, I don't think I ever will.

He's just a really nice guy and we have a lot of fun together when we go out.

He seems as if he would do just about anything for me and I have to admit to you that I like that.

He makes me feel special, pretty, important and he's just so totally sweet and kind to me all of the time. He's just so much fun, so nice, so totally cool ... but definitely not my type of guy and certainly not what I'm looking for when it comes to settling down.

But. ... I don't want to settle either!

**F**irst of all, I think you need to seriously take a nice, long time-out and reevaluate exactly what prefabricated standards and prerequisites you're using to determine what sort of guy you do and don't want in your life.

Honestly, my dear, if I might dare to be so bold and honest with you, it sounds to me like you aren't currently dealing with a full deck, basing your cues on what Mr. Right should be about in order to make you happy!

Lets see: he's really nice, lots of fun, sincerely caring and affectionate toward you, generous, kind, sees you as his ideal woman and actually makes you feel really good about yourself and happy when you're with him!

Hmm, yeah, I can definitely see what your problem is with this loser.

Wow! No wonder you're in such a hurry to cast him aside and blow him out of your life, so that you can make room for some dude who will come along and treat you like crap, not care about your feelings and lower your self-esteem, while creating a lot of stress, tension, frustration and drama in your life.

You definitely strike me as a woman who has her head on straight, knows what she wants and has her priorities well organized!

Mary, honestly—are you kidding me?

Right now there are 1,000 other women reading this chapter and desperate to figure out how to get in touch with you to get this guy's phone number before some other wise woman sweeps him off his feet with appreciation and respect.

Okay, all kidding aside, you asked me what you should do. So here's what my sincere and honest assessment and suggestion are: stop thinking of spending time with a really nice guy who makes you feel good, appreciates you for who you are and likes to treat you like a *queen* as some sort of a problem.

That's *not* a problem, Mary, except in your head—so let the concept of its being a problem go, and just have a good time with the guy while it lasts.

This really isn't as *complicated* as you seem to have made it out to be. I mean, sure, it's understandable that you may not ever fall in love with this guy. (That's pretty much true for every other guy who you ever have dated or will ever date, so no biggie there.)

Just leave it at that! Enjoy whatever time you have together, and as long as both of you are having a good time in each other's company, and no one is being held against his or her will or good consciousness, or manipulated into sticking around through false proclamations of love or potential possibilities of love, then there's no problem of the Laws of Love being broken here.

Just make sure there isn't any sort of behind-the-scenes, under-the-radar deceit regarding the possibility of a long-term, permanent relationship—as long as you know that this guy has already been written off as Not Qualified. As long as no one is getting hurt or being lied to here, then there simply isn't any sort of problem worthy of our concern or discussion.

My question to you is, "What makes you so sure he's made up his mind that *you're the one for him,* and that he's really ready to settle down forever with *you* as his perfect woman anyway?" Has he ever actually come out and said that to you, directly to your face?

I only bring this up because I have noticed an increasingly large number of women these days who assume that just because a guy treats them well—shows them a great time and is polite, kind, generous, respectful and caring, and makes them feel good about life and themselves—that he must obviously be in love with them and ready to get married.

Experience tells me that there are actually a *lot* of pretty decent guys out there, if you simply learn where to look and know what you are looking for. I'm sensing that you have had some seriously misguided programming running inside your mind, leading you down a lot of dark and disastrous roads until some valuable life lessons are learned.

My fear for you is that you seem to show all the symptoms of a girl growing up watching garbage TV and junk movies—so you think you need to pursue or allow yourself to be taken by the stereotypical, two-dimensional, cartoon-cutout Bad Boy!

Here's the ridiculously trivial, negative reality that you will eventually learn about wasting your time and constantly getting hurt, used and degraded by the typical Bad Boy. In the simplest terms possible, Bad Boys are two things:

(1) They are *bad*! These guys don't have the capacity or depth to treat you any other way than *badly*, because that's precisely who they are.

(2) They are *boys*!—just a leftover remnant of the 1950s' Peter Pan Principle in which guys refuse to grow up and become men. They hide in the delusional dress-up game of playing the Bad Boy and never have to grow up and accept responsibility for their own lives and actions.

Yep, the Bad Boy definitely sounds like quite a catch and precisely the type of man who will naturally be ready for a serious, committed, long-term relationship. Always a clever and very wise choice from the Menu of Men—at least if you are planning to eat from the Children's Menu!

These guys are just as pathetically silly and delusionally out of touch as the unwitting girls so desperately seeking their attention and company, like moths lured to the flame. The inevitable outcome is that when you play with Bad Boy fire, you are going to get burned—and usually badly.

But I know the drill and realize that in most

cases, there are very few women out there truly ready to think this issue through until they have personally suffered the slings and arrows of a typical Bad Boy Burning. So enough on that particular topic until you write in from the Intensive Care Burn Ward.

 **Simple Solution**

Logic would normally state that as long as the two of you are having a good time together and no one is lying about a promise of probable or potential permanence in the relationship, you ought to carry on until one or both of you goes elsewhere.

However, the disturbing undertones of your comments lead me to think that the very best advice here is for you to let the guy go. Free him up to find the woman who could possibly learn to appreciate and value what you perceive as his odd set of character flaws and personal idiosyncrasies—before somebody gets hurt.

Instinctively, I don't think that it's him who is most vulnerable and likely to get hurt between the two of you. In fact, when the story has played it-self out, you will mostly likely lament turning your back and pushing away perhaps the only man who actually accepted and valued you for who you were and was willing to look past your flaws to see you as wonderful and beautiful. Trust me, I've been that guy to quite a few women.

Clearly in your mind, there's a small voice telling you that there's a chance you could end up spending your entire life alone and empty, so you are drawn to accept the attention of what you mis-takenly perceive as a partial man. In your fears, having at least a partial man in your life is better than being completely alone!

Since you have already decided that this guy should be written off your list, set him free and allow him to go find happiness. Or is there possi-bly the big, dark, inner secret here that you either:

(1) Really, actually like the guy, but because he doesn't match up to the social expectations of the crowd that you are currently hanging out with, you have to pretend that you're not interested in him; or

(2) Really are so afraid you won't ever find

someone right for you that you will hold him back from his happiness and satisfaction in life—because as everybody knows, misery loves company?

Overall, I think there is a very important lesson about respect and tolerance, character and values waiting for you just around the corner, Mary, and I sincerely wish you well.

 *Shelby Says:*

Basically, this feels like an ugly, bad and sticky situation for both of you, so I think you need to break this thing off as soon as humanly possible—with respect, kindness, grace and care.

Keeping the guy around hurts both of your chances of ever finding what you are as individuals independently looking for in a relationship, so prolonging this is only going to be painful for both of you. Let him go and move on.

However, please seriously take a good look at your idea of the Ideal Man before you resume your search for the perfect relationship. Otherwise I feel you could get yourself seriously injured—

physically as well as emotionally, mentally and spiritually.

**...when she's sleeping with two guys at the same time.**

**From Sandy in Miami, FL**

*I never thought this could happen, but here I am in love with two guys at the same time. I don't know what to do about the situation. I don't want to hurt either of them, but the fact is it's taken a toll on me physically and emotionally.*

*What's worst is they don't know about each other. They both complete me and satisfy me in so many ways.*

*Before, I felt lucky, now I feel screwed and cursed.*

L isten, don't ever let anyone tell you it's impossible or even improbable to love two people at the same time. It happens a lot more often than people would assume. Most people just never really bothered to think the entire scenario all the way through, but consider the above as an example.

First of all, there are nearly as many definitions for the word *love* as there are people out there loving other people. For instance, I certainly love my mom, my wife, my sister, my son, my nieces, my nephew and a whole wide assortment of various family members and friends, authors, musicians, inspirational leaders, spiritual guides, etc. Get the picture?

People are specifically designed to love as many people as we possibly can. However, when it comes to romantic or erotic love, things can quite quickly get very *complicated* indeed—when there is more than one recipient of your precious gift of love!

Being *in love* or sleeping with two people may be more common than we expect, but it's most definitely a *complicated* scene. And in fact, the potential for at least one of the love triangle's participant's eventually getting hurt is very high.

Face it: being in love is a totally awesome and powerful feeling, something I believe absolutely everybody should experience at least once, if not multiple times, throughout his or her lifetime. However, experience has taught me that it's probably better if you do it with one person at a time.

Of course, it seems to be more *complicated* to control than one might logically come to expect. You see, if you think being in love is totally awesome and the most wonderful experience in the world, then you are definitely, really going to love the act of initially *falling in love*.

The very term used to describe the experience tells a very interesting tale about just how much control and conscious, cognizant calculation is actually involved in the matter of falling in love. As the word *falling* expresses, it has very little to do with intentional descent or pre-planned design.

With love, we simply *fall* into it—totally unprepared, utterly unwittingly, without any warning or intent at all—like falling into a firepit or right over a cliff.

The experience can often prove to be just as dangerous and painful as falling into a lake or cavern—or over the cliff. Now imagine accidentally falling into a firepit as you are simultaneously falling over a cliff. *Ouch!*

Being in love with two people at the same time is simply too much for anyone to be able to successfully handle or endure for long, which is why it rarely survives more than a few weeks or months at the very longest—and even that short period of time will take its toll, dealing out a fair share of pain and punishment to all concerned!

And that's just considering the emotional aspect of it. When you begin to figure in the effect of adding a sexual component to the equation, the absolute complexity of the scenario begins to multiply exponentially. Soon the various risks and *complications* can only be sufficiently measured out precisely by way of using astronomically elaborate mathematics.

All relationships occur in stages—and there are a lot of stages. There is the initial "I'm interested and want to get to know you" stage. Then there is the "I enjoy and am getting comfortable talking to you" stage. Next is the "I like hanging out with you" stage, the "I think I really am beginning to like you" stage, the "Let's kiss" stage, the "Let's make out" stage, the "Let's make love" stage and the "Wow, that was so awesome, let's keep doing that again and again" stage!

It's a very complex set of dynamics, and a whole lot of intricate, intimate factors come into play—emotionally, mentally, physically, psychologically and even spiritually.

When you add a third person to the equation, the complexity of the possibilities shoots well into a realm that the human mind cannot possibly figure out, calculate, predict or even reasonably guess-timate as to what's going to happen next. So we have no choice but to simply observe what we can from watching the scenario play itself out over time and try to come away with some set of data as to what is most likely going to happen next.

Sadly, as awesome as love between *two* people can be, it seems experience has taught us that the end-result of love among *three* people is precisely the opposite of awesome. In other words, it's a big, huge, sloppy, emotionally draining and painful—and in some cases, physically dangerous—kettle of boiling trouble.

If you're in love with two people at once (depending on which stage you're at with each of these individuals), you could be spinning and swirling through a myriad different circumstances that are widely open to the multiple possible effects of hundreds, if not literally thousands of factors that alter the molecular structure of the relationship moment to moment.

The possibilities are as endless as the number of grains of sand on the beach. I know for certain that I have zero chance of being able to accurately and precisely assess where you are right now. I am equally confident that you don't have any more of a clue as to exactly where you are right now than I do.

Some people feel that falling in love can be as random a response to those people in your environment as simply walking into a laboratory while blindfolded and beginning to arbitrarily mix a bunch of chemicals together: just in order—or disorder—to see what by chance might possibly happen.

Others tend to romantically equate the experience of Being in Love with some sort of universally predestined, predetermined Cosmic Re-connection with their singular, specific, pre-designated Soulmate. So is it truly an act of God or merely a chance occurrence? That's for you to determine for yourself.

The one thing that most people agree on is the idea that when you are truly in love, it's usually considered a one-on-one sport, and the participation of an additional member on the team can quite often lead to trouble faster than you can loudly exclaim the words *Oh, my Go...*

Now, you will notice how careful I have been about making sure that I refer to this collection of lovers as *people* instead of *men*. That is because over the years—more and more often these days—one or more of the participants in a love triangle involving a woman, is, well, another woman.

Our culture's set of sexual mores continues to lose its power over many people's behavior and beliefs. More and more variations are now socially acceptable regarding various lifestyle options. There are a lot more circumstances where a woman is not only in love with more than one person at a time, but actually having sexual relations with more than just one person at a time—sometimes simultaneously, as in literally at the exact same time.

Anyone with a little grasp of human psychology can begin to fathom the multiple possibilities that come into play. By design, people who are physically intimate with one another quite naturally begin to develop emotional connections and affections, even when they initially set out with the intentions of completely avoiding such entanglements.

We tend to begin falling in love with those people with whom we are sleeping. Makes you really stop to reconsider just how potentially dangerous rampant and unrestricted promiscuity can be in a culture—not just physically, but emotionally, psychologically and even spiritually.

So what's a lover to do?

You might want to seriously rethink what love means to you with regards to your first lover. After all, the fact that you have found the need to add another lover to the equation might be a sign—a subconscious signal that you actually aren't in love with Person No. 1. I say this basically because human beings in general are internally designed to pair off into couples, often with the intentions of a monogamous relationship intended to last until death do us part!

The very fact that you are experiencing such deep attraction and feelings for Person No. 2 should make you somewhat suspicious as to whether Person No. 1 is your true *beloved*—or as so many prefer to refer to it: *soulmate*.

Of course, you may be wired differently, and if you don't fit the typical, conventional relationship model, that's cool. But is what you are experiencing really *love* or merely *lust*?

Also, if you truly are drawn to a lifestyle with two lovers, you need to be completely honest with yourself (as well as the others) and admit that you are aware of the natural *complications* that will arise when a relationship is now bogged down with the task of effectively meeting the personal, physical, emotional, psychological, spiritual and sexual needs and expectations of three individuals instead of just two.

Any kid who has been alive and actively interacting with others for more than a few years can easily tell you from his/her thus far very short lifespan of experience that it's a proven fact: that in social interactions two is company and three is a crowd.

That's why everyone in the world over the age of 4 already knows from personal experience to do whatever is necessary to avoid being a third wheel or odd man out.

Even the rule-bending Sexual Revolution and erotic experimentations promoted so strongly in the concept of *free love*—foisted so aggressively into our culture and onto the hip and cool scenes back in the mid-1960s—proved to offer very few of the freedoms it promised. Instead, we had large quantities of broken hearts, emotional stress, psychological fear, jealously and a whole new medical encyclopedia of socially transmittable diseases and chronic-stress disorders.

 ***Simple Solution***

I think the most obvious solution is found in the concept of prevention, in which you wisely avoid any and all circumstances that are likely to place your body, mind, heart and soul in a position where this sort of extremely complex *complication*

is almost assuredly going to arise.

Next, it's probably a really great idea to begin carefully re-evaluating your own personal definition, understanding and expectations about exactly what *love* means to you. It might also be helpful to check in with your lovers to make sure that you fully understand what it is that *they* think is going on—what they are feeling, expecting and believing.

I'm certainly no prude, and I am not the slightest bit homophobic. So if you're expecting me to suggest damnation, brimstone and hell-fire for any of the participants in this three-way love triangle (male or female) then you are most likely going to be disappointed.

However, I am a man of the strongest moral convictions, ethical principles and highest possible honor and respect for other humans who share this planet with me. So while I couldn't care less if you have two guys in bed with you right this moment—or for that matter, two other women, or one of each—that's 100% completely your choice.

But if you are deceitfully sleeping around behind either one of your lovers' backs, lying to them and deceiving them as to what you are doing when you are away from their side, then *shame on you*!

That sort of lying and deceit has nothing to do with love. And if you are secretly cheating on either one of your lovers—or both—and they don't know what's going on, then don't you dare use the word *love*, because you clearly know nothing about what that term means.

If you have secrets that you need to fess up to, then now is the time to clear the air and treat these people who you supposedly claim to love with some much-deserved dignity and respect.

Meanwhile, if everything is clearly out in the open and no one is being lied to, then good for you. To me, it's not so much the importance of who you are playing with but that you have the honor and respect to play fairly, honestly and completely true to the spirit of the agreed-upon rules.

The hard truth is that at least one member of the triangle is always going to feel like the odd person out, getting their feelings hurt and never being truly satisfied as long as Lover No. 1 appears to be spending more time, energy, attention and love on Lover No. 2 or 3—or both!

### Shelby Says:

Hey, you're a talented woman who knows what she wants. Some people like cake and others like ice cream. Then there are those who like both, and there is nothing wrong with that.

Some people say there is a rule that states that you can't have your cake and eat it too, but as far as I'm concerned, if you got your cake or ice cream in a fair and honest manner, it's nobody else's business when, where or who you choose to share your sweet desserts with.

Just remember: eat too much and you may find yourself beginning to gain some unwanted weight; and then keep in mind that the cake and ice cream that we're talking about today bite back. So the delicious *hunted* could just as easily and quickly turn around to become the *hunter*.

*"Bon appétit,"* my friend!

# She Says, It's Complicated...

**...when she's married, with kids, but unhappy with him.**

**From Jane in Nashville, TN**

My husband and I have been married for 17 years. He's 10 years my senior. We have a beautiful 12-year old daughter. The first 5 years of our marriage was fairly decent. Not much to write home about. In fact, home is where I was running from.

Anyway, just before things took a turn in our marriage, I got pregnant. I thought having his baby would make him pay attention to me and we could be a family like I've always wanted. Fat chance! The last 12 years have been miserable.

We never do anything together, we haven't had sex in 8 years and when we did, it was disgusting. I'm only 43 years old and I feel like my life has passed me by. I know this isn't true!

*I want to enjoy the rest of my life but I don't want my daughter to suffer, as she absolutely adores her father.*

*What can I do?*

O kay, this can be a sticky situation. When you're married with kids, there are obviously a lot more important things to seriously concern yourself with than simply worrying about how assets are to be divided up should the marriage eventually collapse into that sad state of marital bankruptcy known as divorce.

I give Jane a lot of credit for emphasizing the importance of ensuring that even if her personal relationship with her husband sadly fades into a dark oblivion, she is already cognizant of the great importance that she does what she can to cooperate where possible to help ensure that her daughter maintains a close, strong, positive and loving relationship with her father.

She certainly shows her understanding that when kids are involved, things like who gets this or that possession and precisely how the money is to be split up take a back seat to the human element. Yes, bills need to be paid and possessions have to be put somewhere, but Priority No. 1 is the living treasures that the marriage combined to create as a team effort of husband and wife, father and mother.

An unfulfilling marriage, with kids in the situation, could very well be the very toughest *complication* of them all. That is why we saved it for last. It is going to take all of our insight, dedication, love, commitment and creative energy to resolve this scenario without the kids' being totally devastated in the process.

Remember: the kids are the *only* truly innocent parties involved in this situation. You may claim on the one hand that *he* is a cruel, selfish, manipulative, cold, heartless jerk, and on the other hand that *you* are practically an angel, serving as the loving, caring, sacrificing wife who does everything possible to hold the family together—and that may be very close to the actual truth of the matter.

But even if Hubby is 95% responsible for all of the problems, you still have to fess up to your 5% of the mess to be responsible for—as well as a fair share in the responsibility for agreeing to marry the monster and then ineffectively building up a marriage that doesn't even have the strength to stand up under its own weight.

I'm not pointing fingers or placing blame on anyone, because I'm not there in the middle of your particular situation. All I know is what you told me about the scenario; and the odds of my ever actually hearing his side of the story are slim to none.

The truth is that only *you* can ever really know for sure whether or not you actually tried to make the marriage work and honestly gave it your all to save the marriage. Anyway, as you already know, I'm not here to take sides except that of the kids— because, after all, they're the only completely innocent ones in the whole messy matter.

Only the children stand utterly vulnerable and helpless in this scenario, having absolutely no say or control in the arrangement. And it usually turns out to be the kids who are the most vulnerable victims in a nasty divorce. Whether those injuries are emotional, mental, physical or spiritual, it's the little ones who tend to get hurt when a family comes crashing down.

Other than that, I'm not here to choose either *partner*'s side, but simply to help you find your way out of the *complications* to find the best possible solution for all concerned.

 **Simple Solution**

Look, the fact is that a truly bad marriage simply isn't good for anyone, including the kids. Fighting, yelling, screaming, arguing and any explosive acts of actual or perceived violence, threats, anger, disrespect, fear and the general sense of stress, tension and misery are all part of an awful environment in which to try to successfully raise and bring up well-balanced, happy kids.

So what is the answer? Well, every case is unique, but if you are totally positive that there is definitely nothing left to do that could possibly work to save the marriage, then you probably are better off ending it once and for all—but on terms that are specifically designed to mutually ensure that Priority No. 1 is protecting the kids.

That means no more yelling and screaming; no more fits of anger and the throwing of tizzies; no threats, no physical eruptions, no fear, no blow-ups.

For the sake of the kids, Mom and Dad need to both agree to get on the same page and give the children lots and lots of love, attention, answers, reassurance, encouragement, smiles, hugs, kisses and hope.

Kids simply can't understand things in adult terms, so it is very likely that they will be going through highly emotional periods during which they may alternate between phases of withdrawing inside of themselves and quietly disappearing for a while into their own sullen silence.

Then just as quickly, they may suddenly explode with aggressive fits of stress, tension, anxiety and anger over the fact that their entire world is being torn apart by their parents, while they helplessly and vulnerably sit by and can do nothing to prevent the destruction of their world!

As long as you are constantly communicating with them, reassuring them and answering their numerous questions in such a way as to not try to turn them against their dad or make him the bad guy, then you should do fine. Nevertheless, it's going to be a lot of work with a huge learning curve, so prepare to be completely overwhelmed at first. Just have faith and never give up.

Both parents must do everything in their power to make the transition as smooth and comfortable as possible with lots of communication and love. Be sure to allow the children to regularly see Mom and Dad working at peace together, smiling, happy, cooperative and calmly composed and comfortable for the kids to be around.

 *Warning!*

**Here's what you absolutely cannot do:**
You cannot, under any condition, ever use your children as pawns or tools to hurt your soon-to-be ex. I am not normally one to comfortably or freely toss the word *evil* around, but those parents who use their kids as tools or weapons to hurt, manipulate or control their ex are the foulest kind of evil imaginable. If you ever begin to seriously contem-

plate doing so, stop and seek help immediately!

Pray, meditate, go for a mind-clearing, soul-cleansing walk. Call a friend, go to church—do whatever it takes to stop yourself—because when you eventually realize the terrible damage that such actions inflict on your innocent babies, you will be horrified by your actions. But it won't matter anymore then, *because the damage will already be done.*

Simply don't do it, and seek immediate help or counsel should you ever even briefly consider this catastrophic form of child abuse. No matter how convenient it may momentarily seem, when it comes to controlling and keeping a lid on your kids, never be so cruel as to ever, even for a moment, believe that they are somehow responsible for the divorce.

Remember: kids simply can't possibly understand, successfully ferret out the truth or comprehend the vast complexities of adult situations. And because children's minds are young and the world is still so new to them, they naturally tend to think in patterns that are very self-oriented. Kids see themselves as the very center of their own universe. This means it is only natural for them to begin to wonder if they are somehow responsible for the collapse of the family and Mom or Dad's going away and leaving them and their home.

I hate to think this is even a possible human behavior, but sadly, I have known of parents who have used this common, childish tactic to manipulate and control their children—by falsely assigning them the responsibility for the collapsed marriage and warning them that if they don't behave as they have been told, Dad might not ever come back home.

Hearing of the effects of these horror stories has put tears in my eyes and caused my fists to clench and my hands to shake uncontrollably.

**Warning:** The tender, innocent, fragile and vulnerable hearts, minds, souls and spirits of trusting children who love *both* of their parents—and are panicked and frightened that they may have caused the dissolution of their family and world—are *not* the appropriate dumping ground for parental frustrations, stresses and tensions.

Weigh your words wisely and remember that what you *don't* say is quite often even more damaging than what you *do* say.

It is absolutely imperative that you continually comfort and reassure your children that they are totally innocent and without fault or any responsibility for Mom and Dad's not being able to successfully keep the family together.

Life has plenty of emotionally scarring burdens awaiting your little ones—don't ever allow yourself to weaken to the temptation of using their wondrous, trusting innocence against them. If you ever stooped that low in life, you would never be able to forgive yourself.

Additionally, be sure to stay in constant and consistent communication with the kids to keep a watchful eye and ear as to what exactly Dad, Grandma, Grandpa, Uncle, Aunt, Cousin, etc. are saying about the situation. Sadly, I have been shocked and disgusted to find out what some normal, decent, loving, caring people will suddenly lower themselves to in the middle of a divorce! So most definitely be sure to keep your eyes and ears open and constantly talk to the kids about what they are hearing and being told.

### *Shelby Says:*

Just as you must never use your kids as pawns, weapons or tools to hurt or manipulate their dad, you should also never use the kids as an excuse to stay in a terrible, destructive marriage.

Kids are extremely resilient, and as long as you take some carefully considered steps to ensure that they understand to the very best of their ability what's going on—and that you continually talk with them and give assurances that everything is going to be okay—the kids will come out of this process safely, sanely and securely.

Meanwhile, forcing them to continually endure the craziness of an ugly marriage—with the fighting, yelling, threats, anger, and the potential for violence—only creates circumstances that cause fear, insecurity, anger, alternating blowups and withdrawal that can damage the heart, mind, soul and spirit of your children permanently.

Raising kids in those conditions is a form of child abuse. If the marriage simply can't be saved, then definitely move on—but with the children's well-being continuously Priority No. 1.

# in closing

*C*ongratulations! You have passed through a myriad of topics and concerns in a very direct, sincere and frank manner. You truly deserve a lot of credit for coming forward and being willing to step up to handle all of these very complex and *complicated* subjects with a fully authentic vulnerability and dedicated commitment to finally finding the solutions to your particular situations, as well as the various scenarios that your friends, close associates and family members may be currently struggling through.

This has been a very deep and powerful personal journey, and you may discover that you need to come back from time to time to go over some of the material as a sort of refresher course.

I hope that you have found my insights and methodology extremely helpful to your personal needs and circumstances. I pride myself in being willing to always be completely truthful—telling it exactly as it is, holding nothing back and never sugar-coating or watering down the truth.

I've been working in this specialized field of endeavor for over 20 years now. What women truly need is *not* to be protected from the truth or carried across the ravines, but instead allowed to gather, display and exert their own amazing strength and inner power—qualities that, as a man, I can only view with total awe and respect, admiration and relish.

If at times I seemed a bit too blunt or direct, please understand that there are some really uncomfortable, creepy and crappy things going on out there in this great big world of ours. And really, the most effective way of dealing with it all is to do so directly—head on with no holds barred and no punches held back.

If you have a friend or family member who needs to face these matters directly without shrinking or shirking personal responsibility— where a woman is now perfectly capable of taking complete control of her own life, without any fear, excuse, or embarrassment—then please share a little bit of our conversation with them and invite them to come along for the next journey, as we venture further and further into the deepest, most wondrously exciting and mysterious territories found on earth: *you*!

It's been my honor and privilege to serve as your trusted guide, and I greatly look forward to our next trip to the innermost levels of awareness, consciousness, self-expansion and self-reliance, as well as conflict resolution and personal-solution discovery!

Till then, be the very best *you* that you can possibly be, and remember: nobody can do you better than you can yourself!

Be strong and be empowered.

~Shelby M. Hill

# simple tips
## to avoid complicated situations with men

## Don't be a Desperate Diane

Men can be wolves—yes, sometimes they travel in packs—and they can sense when you are weak and eager to please them...in any capacity.

## Ask questions!

Men typically get uncomfortable when women ask too many questions. Seriously! I mean don't just ask empty questions. Ask questions that elicit insight into his interest in you and what his motives are. For example: never ask a guy, "Why do you like me?" That's too easy to get around. He will simply shower you with broad compliments —and you most likely will not feel any more special than his sister would be hearing the same words. Ask him a question like, "How long has it been since you've had a meaningful relationship, and what exactly happened to end it?"

## Carry yourself like a woman

You already carry yourself as a woman at all times; be sure he treats you accordingly. Just because you're interested in him doesn't mean the quality of who you are is diminished. Otherwise, he'll lose respect—and the table will be one-sided, leaving you feeling more for him than he does for you.

## Really...don't give it up so fast

I know people will tell you that it doesn't matter, but often, those situations are the exception, not the rule. Don't be the rule.

## Background checks are GOOD!

Say what you want, but modern society requires that you know as much as you can about a person without necessarily violating him—but definitely protecting yourself. I'm not suggesting spending $29.99 for a thorough FBI check, but asking around about the guy? Absolutely! Ask your friends. Determine what social circle he frequents and casually ask about him there. You'll be surprised what you find. People like talking about others and you can use this to your advantage.

## Don't lie to yourself

Be honest with yourself about what it is you're looking for in terms of a relationship. If you know you're not looking for love, then do not act that way. If you're really just looking to have fun, then behave that way—but don't convince yourself you feel something you really aren't ready for. Regardless of your reasons, be honest with yourself.

## Understand your expectations and make sure he's clear as well

Knowing your expectations for getting involved with someone is crucial, because it's easy to re-prioritize and lose your true focus—which should be *you*. Know that you're expecting to be in a relationship and you don't want a sex thing, but at the same time, you don't want to rush things.

## Listen to what he is NOT saying

When attracted to a man, it's common that everything he says seems like golden whispers to your ears. Most guys know how to say the right things at the right time to get the Right Response. But here's where you have to be sharp. He's always going to say the *right* thing—it's your responsibility to pay attention to hear what's not being said. Read between the lines. And no matter how good it may sound, there may be more to it that isn't as genuine as you would like it to be. This is typically identifiable through his actions or lack of them.

## Challenge him

Men don't expect to be challenged when they "lay down the rules," or when they tell you what they are going to do or not do. Most men feel like, "Hey, this is what I said, and that's final." My suggestion is that if it doesn't sound right or feel right to you, don't be afraid to challenge him. If he gets mad and wants to break up, he's doing you a favor.

## Pulse check

I always recommend that during your dating experience with a man, it's important to do a "pulse check" to see where he stands. And let him know where you stand in terms of the relationship. This is incredibly helpful, because it minimizes confusion about where the relationship is going.

## Pin him down and hold him accountable

If you don't hold him accountable, then he'll walk all over you—plain and simple.

## Get clarity about his expectations

Men have a knack for skirting around direct questions. They are quite capable of offering vague, meaningless answers that hold absolutely no weight.

## Is he fresh out of the "relationship womb?"

If he's newly single, don't run, but briskly walk away. Most often, regardless of what he says, you are a rebound. Just do yourself a favor and keep it friendly unless you're in the same situation as he is—then you have something in common. More than likely, you'll be paying the price for what the last woman did or did not do to him.

## Who has he dated?

Do you know someone he's dated—or someone who knows someone he's dated? Find out how he's managed those past relationships. Most likely—if only a short time has passed (one to three years)—he likely has *not* changed.

## Umm...so he doesn't like to talk about things

*Red flag!* This is the lamest excuse that most men hide behind when they are trying to conceal something or just don't feel the same as you do. If he says he doesn't like to talk about things, trust me: you will always be in the dark. I can assure you that when there's something that's bothering him, he'll be sure to let you know all about it. Avoid this situation as soon as you can.

## What's his 1-, 2-, 3- ,4- , 5-year plan?

Let's face it: it's not all about his taking care of you but it *is* definitely about what the future holds. Can he contribute equally to it? If he doesn't have 2- and 5-year plans for his life, then he still has some growing to do in order to organize his priorities. Your objective in life should not be to financially support a man for the rest of his life. This can make for a backwards *complicated* situation.

## Don't try to make a heart fit into a triangle

What I'm saying here is that you're a smart woman. You're in tune with yourself enough to know if you're compatible with someone, so please don't try to make it work when you already know that it really can't. Sure, he may look good and he may be financially secure. But chemistry is very important in a successful relationship and you have to recognize this. Do the right thing for *you* first and foremost.

## Can he talk?

You may be laughing about this, but look: if a guy has poor conversation skills or poor articulation, for the most part, he's poor in other aspects of his life. You'll be selling yourself short *if* you want a certain caliber of man.

## He is the company he keeps

Men roll in packs, so pay close attention to his friends. If they are disrespectful to women or are womanizers, drunks, thugs, players, etc., remember: they're his friends because they have a lot in common.

## Insecurity leads to insanity

An oversized ego is the very first sign of insecurity. So, please stroke his ego, tell him nice things about himself and let him know that he's too good for you. He's so good that you don't deserve him— humbly break it off. If you don't, get ready to make it all about him all of the time!

# warning signs
## that don't lie...
## key indicators that he's complicated

The challenge about *complicated* situations with men is that they can be camouflaged. The key is knowing what to look for and how to pay attention when the signs begin to surface. If it's not a good situation, believe me: the signs will surface.

Following are some serious Warning Signs that serve as a heads-up about this guy and are not to be ignored. In fact, if any of these are causing your eyes to widen really big—and you're losing your breath because you're in a current *complicated* situation—please strongly consider putting your Exit Strategy in play as soon as possible.

### Warning! Red Alert!
### Warning! Please Bail Out!

*If he has any type of addiction to sex, pornography, alcohol, drugs, etc.* Bail out! Any addictions are sure-fire signs that lead to a difficult relationship.

*If he is overly emotionally expressive in a very short period of time.* For example, if you've been dating about a month or so and he's telling you he's in love with you and can't ever see you out of his life, ask for the check and call a cab. There's a great level of co-dependency that is lurking around the corner in that relationship if you choose to go any further.

*If he is verbally or physically abusive to himself, his friends or you.* Please don't waste your time. This isn't going to change—he has little respect for himself, much less you.

*If he shows signs of being hot-tempered.* Get completely out of his way by never calling him again.

*If he is controlling and everything has to be his way*

*or the highway*. Take the highway. You'll lose your sense of self very quickly in this relationship. His motive is to break you down and make you subservient to him.

⚠ *If he is jealous of your friends—male or female.* Choose your friends every time. If you don't, you will inevitably isolate yourself from those who care most about you. In a short time, you will be subjected to more jealous, dominating behavior. You will feel trapped!

⚠ *If he is not definitive about his relationship status, in other words, waffling about whether he's single technically or legally.* Wrap up the conversation as soon as you can and tell him to look you up when he's man enough to make a decision.

⚠ *If he is dishonest early on in the relationship.* This is a pretty good sign that more lies are to come. Cut your losses now—you don't have time for the games.

⚠ *If he is very capable of working and taking care of himself but still lives at home with his parents.* What's wrong with that picture?

⚠️ *If he has a tough time looking you in the eye when he speaks to you.* There's no doubt about it: he's hiding something.

⚠️ *If he is very capable of working and taking care of himself but unemployed and not really looking.* You should keep looking, too—elsewhere.

# second thoughts
## thinking of staying
## because it's complicated?

You're going to want to stay or go back to him. Over the years, I've coached and shared advice with many women who are in *complicated* situations with men. I have shared only a few of the most common situations in this first volume.

The most consistent thread running through each of their situations—no matter how common or strange the situation—it was always hard for her to leave him. It's never that you don't understand the situation, it's really about how you get out of it without being an emotional wreck, hurting yourself or the children, and hoping you're not making a mistake. Although the situation isn't the best, you're still filled with hope that perhaps one day soon—or next week or next month—the situation will change and he will suddenly awake one morning and be everything you hoped he would be.

Or he's changed and he stopped drinking, abusing you, cheating on you or lying to you. Miraculously, he's changed. I have yet to see a case with such a turnaround unless there's been a high level of outer support to treat the core issues of his addiction or habitual detrimental habits, such as lying or cheating.

So you leave him. You're fed up for the 13th time and you go back to him. You're having second thoughts that you know are wrong! This is when you have to somehow look at the situation from a different angle, because the previous one is not showing you anything different. And that's why you keep going back. This is the time to figure out what you really want and what's best for you.

Is the pain of staying greater than the pain of going? Or is the gain from leaving worth so much that you can't see it any other way except *you must move on with your life?*

# checklist
## your "Me" Priority Checklist (MPC)

*Un-complicate your life!* You're going to go through an ocean of emotions during a *complicated* relationship. At some point, you have to know when enough is enough and how to determine an exit strategy.

I know it may sound like you're preparing for combat but, the truth is that you sort of *are*. You have to get in the right state of mind that says you are getting out and there's no turning back. It's not only a *complicated* situation but it's an unhealthy one too—on so many levels.

Now that I've reminded you of the seriousness of your situation, let's lay some ground work for your departure.

Given the current circumstances, your priorities are probably disorganized right now, or your feelings for him—or both. Although even at this juncture, you're probably still on the fence about whether you should leave or not—I'm here to give you a *big* nudge! But first, I need you to do a little more soul-searching. Please understand that I can tell you what I think may be best for you, but ultimately it's your decision. If I tell you what to do, it will do absolutely nothing to sustain change and repel you from this situation and similar ones in the future.

In other words, I need your buy-in! If you don't believe that this is not a good situation for you—or maybe it's you and your children—then you're only going to end up right back here a few days, a week or a month from now.

Let's complete the following exercises and see where you stand once we tally the results. Okay? Okay!

The following chart lists common priorities with which women are faced when making the decision to leave a *complicated* situation. To the right of each item are numbers reflecting a scale of importance from 1 (less important) to 3 (more important) to 5 (most important). Individually mark the number that matches your personal concerns and then compare. When done, count the number of 1s, 2s, 3s, etc. If you have more 5s than any other number, then your decision is clear and you should consider taking action towards those priorities.

Your Name

## ME Priority Checklist

| | | | | | |
|---|---|---|---|---|---|
| Family/Parenting | 1 | 2 | 3 | 4 | 5 |
| Money/Savings | 1 | 2 | 3 | 4 | 5 |
| Debts/Assets | 1 | 2 | 3 | 4 | 5 |
| Career/Profession | 1 | 2 | 3 | 4 | 5 |
| Spiritual Awareness | 1 | 2 | 3 | 4 | 5 |
| Health/Aging | 1 | 2 | 3 | 4 | 5 |
| Social Relationships | 1 | 2 | 3 | 4 | 5 |
| Personal Development | 1 | 2 | 3 | 4 | 5 |
| Entertainment | 1 | 2 | 3 | 4 | 5 |